Classifying Living Things

How Organisms Are Related

DEVELOPED IN COOPERATION

WITH

THE INDIANAPOLIS ZOO

INDIANAPOLIS, INDIANA

Copyright © 1995 by Scholastic Inc.   All rights reserved. Published by Scholastic Inc.   Printed in the U.S.A.
ISBN 0-590-27610-7
5 6 7 8 9 10   09   01 00 99 98 97 96

LIVING THINGS ARE DIVERSE,
INTERDEPENDENT, AND EVOLVING.

Classifying Living Things

Organisms can be classified into groups
based on similar structures.

Read-Aloud

Classifying Living Things

Living organisms can be grouped into five large kingdoms.

Literature

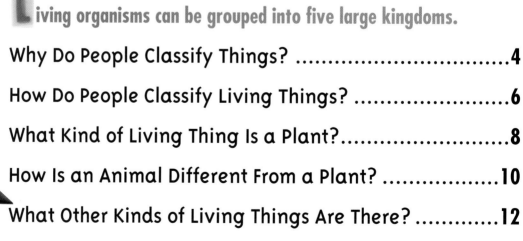

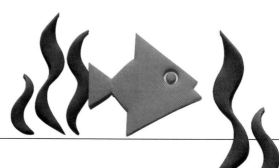

Literature

The smallest classification group is a species.

Why Do People Classify Things?

Suppose you wanted to try a new breakfast cereal. Where in the grocery store would you look for it? Most grocery store items are grouped by certain characteristics—things such as the kind of food they are or the way they're packaged. How does that help people shop?

What kinds of things do you put in groups at home and at school? How do you group them?

Which store would you rather shop in? Why?

Organize a school store.

1 Have each team member pick five different objects in the classroom.

2 Decide on a characteristic you can use to sort all the items your team has picked. Then divide the items into two or three groups. Give each group a name.

3 Now divide your groups into smaller groups and name them. How many ways did you and your classmates find to group the objects?

When you put objects into groups, you classify them. People classify things in different ways for different reasons. Most often people classify things by what they're used for and how they're made. What other objects can you classify?

You need:
Classroom objects

THINK!
Why do people divide big groups into smaller ones?

How Do People Classify Living Things?

When you go into a store, you can find what you want because everything is classified into groups. People even classify living things.

Living things are called organisms, and there are millions of kinds on Earth. How many kinds do you see in this picture? How would you classify them?

You need:
Trading cards
Index cards

Classify some organisms.

❶ Look at the organisms on your trading cards. How are they alike? How are they different?

❷ Pick a characteristic and use it to sort the organisms into big groups. Now divide the big groups into smaller groups. Make a table or drawing to show your plan.

❸ Draw a trading card for yourself. Which group would you put it in? Do you need to change your groups?

❹ Now compare your classification with those of your classmates. How many different characteristics did you use to group the organisms?

THINK!
How many different characteristics can you think of for classifying organisms?

Scientists classify organisms by such characteristics as body parts and ways of getting food. They divide the organisms into big groups called <u>kingdoms</u>. Each kingdom is divided into many smaller groups. But as scientists learn more about an organism, they may classify it in a different group.

What Kind of Living Thing Is a Plant?

Scientists used to classify organisms into just two kingdoms—plants and animals. But they've learned a lot about organisms and have also found many more. So now most scientists use five kingdoms. The plant kingdom is one of the biggest.

What exactly is a plant? How does it get what it needs to survive?

You need:
Tape
Plastic cups
Markers or crayons
Soil
Water
Seeds
ThinkMat 4
Trading cards

Meadow plants

Compare plants.

1 Label six cups. Put water in 1 and 4, and put soil in 2, 3, 5, and 6. Sprinkle 15 seeds in each cup.

2 Put cups 1, 2, and 3 in a dark place. Put 4, 5, and 6 in a sunny place. Predict which seeds will grow best.

3 Water the soil in cups 3 and 6 every day. Keep a table of what you see each day.

4 After one week, decide which cup has the healthiest plants. Draw what a healthy plant looks like, and label its parts. Be sure to include its roots. What do plants need to survive?

5 Now find all the plant pictures on your trading cards. How are they like your plants? How are they different?

THINK!
How would you classify the meadow plants into smaller groups?

How Is an Animal Different From a Plant?

Daisies and grass and pine trees all belong to the plant kingdom. They and all other plants share some characteristics. Bears and fish and crickets all belong to the animal kingdom. Because they're all animals, they must be alike in some ways. How are members of the animal kingdom alike?

Discover what animals do.

1 Make a place for your cricket to live. Make sure it has air, water, and food.

2 Look at your cricket with the hand lens. Observe the cricket's behavior. How does it move? How does it respond to changes around it? How does it eat? What else does it do?

3 Compare your observations of the cricket with what you know about other animals. How is the cricket like those animals?

4 Now look at your trading cards and decide which ones show animals.

Compare your cricket with what you know about plants. How is your cricket different from a plant? How are all animals different from plants? How are they the same? Knowing that an organism is an animal tells you a lot about it. What do you think makes an animal an animal?

You need:
Container with cover
Sand
Water holder
Cricket food
Cricket
Hand lens
Trading cards

THINK! How is the cricket like you?

What Other Kinds of Living Things Are There?

You probably see some plants and animals every day. But most members of the other three kingdoms are much harder to see. What are they like?

Meet the fungi kingdom.

1 Stick tape on your bag and mark off 20 cm, as the picture shows. Put in the cereal and yeast. Then add a little warm water.

2 Squeeze the air out and zip the bag. Roll the top of the bag down as far as you can. What's the highest number showing on the tape?

3 Put the bag in warm water and observe what happens. In 10 minutes, remove the bag and roll the top down again. What changes do you observe?

As the yeast used the sugar in the cereal, the yeast made a gas. When yeast is used in breads, it makes gas in the dough. What do you think that gas would do to the bread?

You need:
Plastic bag
Tape
Ruler
Marker
4 spoons of cereal
1 spoon of yeast
Warm water
Hand lens
Pan
Plastic cup

Members of the fungi kingdom include yeasts, mushrooms, and molds. In nature, fungi help break down the bodies of dead organisms so their nutrients can go back to the soil. Most fungi grow best in dark places. How is that different from the way plants grow?

Some fungi are so tiny that you'd need a hand lens or microscope to see them. Members of the moneran and protist kingdoms include the very smallest organisms. These pictures show you what two of them look like through a microscope. How are they different from the plants and animals you know?

This organism—magnified about 500 times—is a protist. All protists live in wet areas.

These Bacteria—magnified about 20,000 times—are monerans.

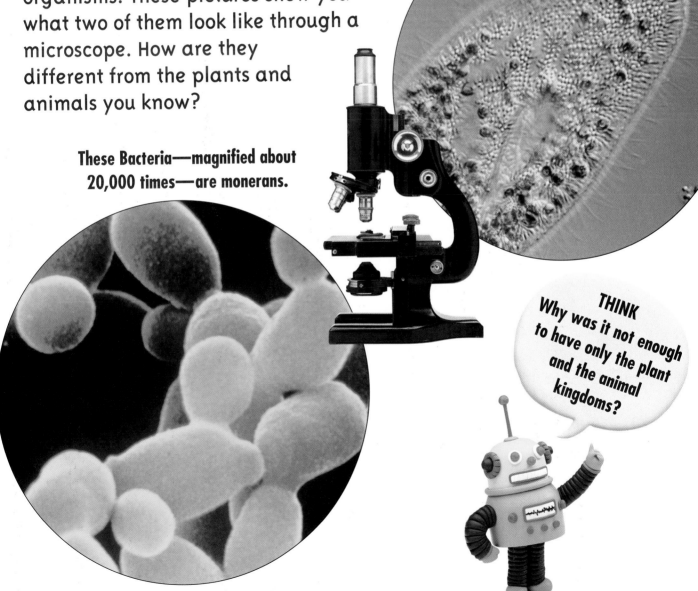

THINK
Why was it not enough to have only the plant and the animal kingdoms?

How Are Animals Classified Into Smaller Groups?

Each kingdom includes thousands of kinds of organisms. The animal kingdom has the most kinds of all, and there are big differences among animals. A clam and a cat are both animals, so you know how they're alike. What are some of their differences?

One way people classify animals is by whether or not they have backbones. Animals that have backbones are <u>vertebrates</u>. They have skeletons inside their bodies. Animals without backbones are <u>invertebrates</u>.

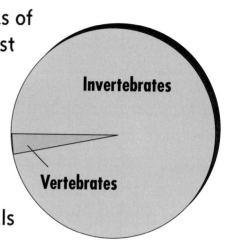

Which group is bigger?

VERTEBRATES

Tiger   Bluebird   Tortoise   Newt

INVERTEBRATES

Scallop   Bee   Worm   Jellyfish

Classify animals.

1 What differences can you see among the animals in the pictures?

2 Look at your cricket. It has a thin body shell instead of a skeleton. Which group would you put it in?

3 Use these pictures to help you predict which animals on your cards are vertebrates and which are invertebrates.

4 Feel your partner's back. Which group do you and your partner belong to?

How would you classify vertebrates and invertebrates into smaller groups?

You need:
Cricket in a home
Hand lens
Trading cards

Snapper

Sponge   Sea star

THINK!
How could you move if you didn't have a skeleton?

What's the Biggest Group of Invertebrates?

If you've ever sat for a while on a patch of grass or sand, you probably saw a lot of animals crawling around. Some might even have crawled on you. What were they like?

It's safe to say that most of those animals belonged to the same group of invertebrates. In fact, more than three-fourths of all kinds of animals are members of that group. They're called <u>arthropods</u>.

If you study these pictures, you'll see what all arthropods have in common. Look at the ant's legs and the way its head and body parts are put together. All the arthropods have bodies made up of two or more parts called segments.

CHARACTERISTICS OF ARTHROPODS

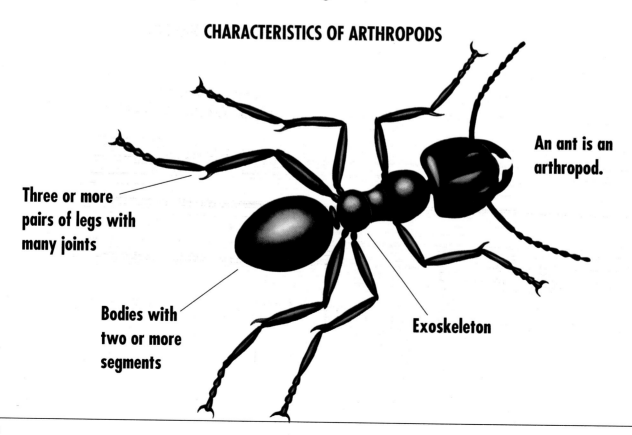

Three or more pairs of legs with many joints

An ant is an arthropod.

Bodies with two or more segments

Exoskeleton

When an arthropod sheds its exoskeleton, it waits for the new one to dry and stiffen.

You know that arthropods don't have backbones or skeletons like yours. Instead, they have hard outer coverings, or <u>exoskeletons</u>, that protect them like suits of armor. Some kinds of arthropods have harder exoskeletons than others.

If you lived in a suit of armor, what would you do when you started to grow? The dragonfly pictures show what all the arthropods do as they grow.

THINK!
What problems could happen when an arthropod sheds its exoskeleton?

How Are Arthropods Classified Into Smaller Groups?

Did you know that a butterfly is more like a crab than like a bird? That's because a bird is a vertebrate, and butterflies and crabs are invertebrates. They're both arthropods, too. What does that tell you about each animal?

There are so many kinds of arthropods that scientists have divided them into nine smaller groups. These pictures show animals from four of the groups. How are they different from one another?

A centipede is a chilopod. Chilopods have poison on their front claws that help them catch their food.

A wasp is an insect. Most insects have wings, and many live in social groups.

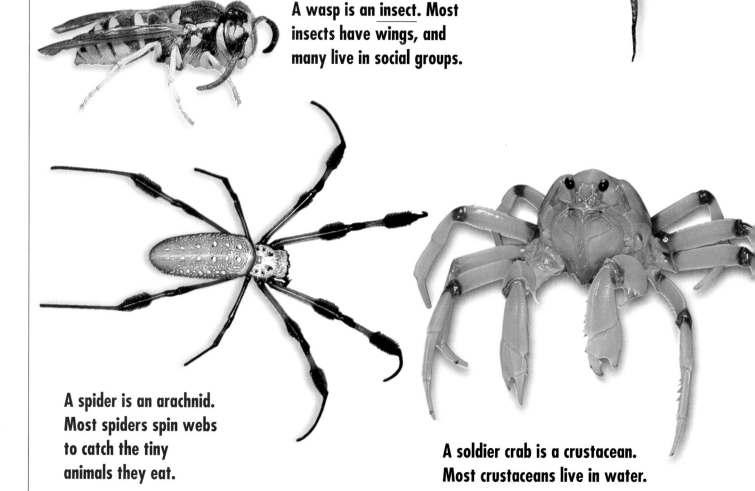

A spider is an arachnid. Most spiders spin webs to catch the tiny animals they eat.

A soldier crab is a crustacean. Most crustaceans live in water.

Compare arthropods.

1 Look carefully at the arthropods in these pictures.
- How many legs do they have?
- How many body parts do they have?
- How are their bodies shaped?
- Do they have wings?
- Do they have antennae?

2 Make a table to compare the arthropods. Which group does your cricket belong to? How do you know?

3 Pick the cards showing arthropods from your invertebrate trading cards. Try to classify them into these groups of arthropods.

You need:
Cricket in a home
Hand lens
Paper
Markers or crayons
Trading cards

THINK!
Why aren't spiders classified as insects?

How Are Insects Classified?

Insects make up the biggest group of arthropods. About a million different kinds have been discovered! All insects have three sets of legs and three main body parts. But how are they different?

Investigate insect mouth parts.

1 Tear part of the paper into tiny bits. Wet the rest of the paper and put it in a dish; then cover the dish with plastic. Put sugar water in another dish and plain water in a bottle. These are your models of insect foods.

2 Cut the straight straw into a pointed one. Attach the sponge to one clothespin. With the straw that bends and the other clothespin, you have four models of insect mouths.

3 Predict which mouth part will work best on each model food. Then test them. Make a table to compare your results.

You need:
Paper towels
Sugar water
2 dishes
Plastic wrap
Bottle
Straws
Scissors
2 clothespins
Sponge

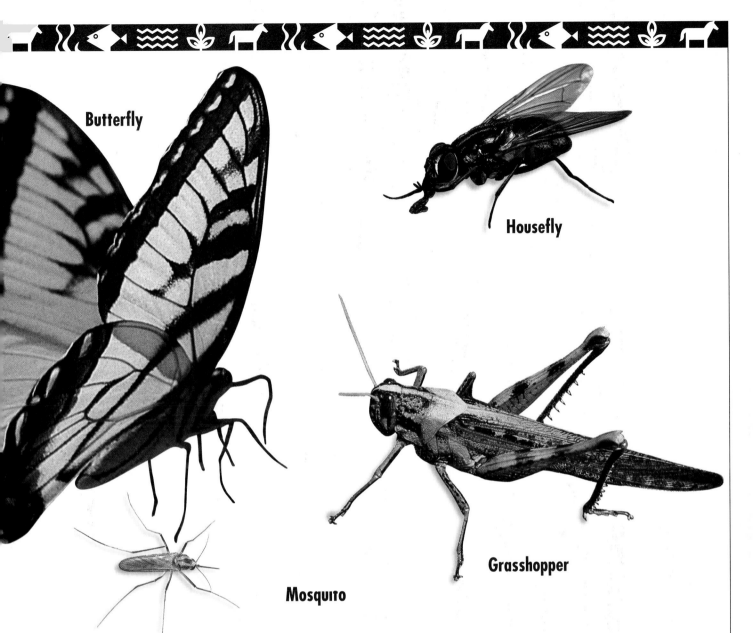

Butterfly

Housefly

Grasshopper

Mosquito

Different kinds of insects eat different foods. They have special mouth parts for their own types of food. Houseflies slurp up sweet, mushy foods. Grasshoppers chew on leaves. Butterflies sip nectar from flowers. Mosquitoes suck blood from other animals. What kind of mouth do you think would work best for each kind of insect?

Different groups of insects have other differences, too. Look closely at these pictures. How do you think long hind legs help an insect? What other differences do you see?

THINK!
Which insect mouth model is most like your cricket's mouth?

What Are Warm-Blooded Vertebrates ?

You saw how invertebrates are classified into many groups. Vertebrates are classified into five groups. Two groups, birds and mammals, are <u>warm-blooded</u>.

Being warm-blooded means that an animal's body temperature stays the same most of the time, whether it's warm or cold outside. How could that help an animal survive?

You need:
Hand lens
Feathers
Paper
Water
Trading cards

Compare their covers.

❶ Examine a feather. Gently separate the sections, then smooth them together. What part allows this to happen?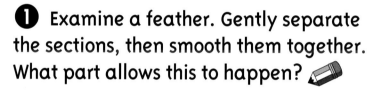

❷ Look at a hair from your head and hair on your arm. How is hair different from a feather? How is hair on your head different from arm hair?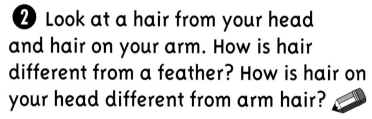

❸ Drip some water on the feather, your arm, and the paper. How are they all different?

❹ Now look at your trading cards. Find the vertebrates that have feathers. They're birds. Find the vertebrates that have fur or hair. They're mammals. How else are these groups different?

All birds hatch from eggs. But not all birds fly. Penguins use their wings like flippers to swim. How can you tell they're birds?

Mammal mothers make milk for their babies. Like these deer, most mammals live on land, but some—like whales and sea lions—live in water.

Only birds have feathers. All vertebrates with fur or hair are mammals. Even whales have a few bristly hairs. Look at the pictures to see how feathers and fur cover each animal. How do you think these coverings help birds and mammals stay warm in winter?

THINK!
What kinds of mammals do you see every day?

What Are Cold-Blooded Vertebrates?

Warm-blooded animals can move around better in cold weather than <u>cold-blooded</u> animals can. Being cold-blooded means that an animal's body temperature changes with the temperature of the air or water around it.

Reptiles, amphibians, and fish are cold-blooded vertebrates. How else are they different from mammals and birds?

You need:
ThinkMat 14
Scissors
Hole Punch
Pipe cleaner
Trading cards

Sort by characteristics.

❶ Cut out cards. Punch the holes, and cut out the shaded areas.

❷ Use the list of characteristics on the Master Card to make a table for all five vertebrate groups.

❸ Stack all cards to face the same way. Push a pipe cleaner through hole 1. Shake the cards. Most vertebrates left on the pipe cleaner lay eggs. Check them off on your table.

❹ Repeat step 3 for each of the other holes. Complete your table.

❺ Find the reptiles, amphibians, and fish in your trading cards. How are they different from one another?

COLD-BLOODED VERTEBRATES

Frogs, salamanders, and toads are amphibians. Their skin can be dry or moist, bumpy or smooth. Almost all amphibians begin their lives in water.

Lizards, turtles, snakes, and crocodiles are reptiles. Some reptiles live in water; some live in deserts. Most of them lay soft, leathery eggs on land.

Some fishes—like this trout— have harder skeletons than others. Most fishes are coated with overlapping scales that protect them. Most fishes lay eggs.

THINK! What kind of vertebrate are you?

During cold winters and very hot summers, reptiles and amphibians stay hidden underground. They sleep there until the weather becomes comfortable, and then they are active again.

What Is a Species?

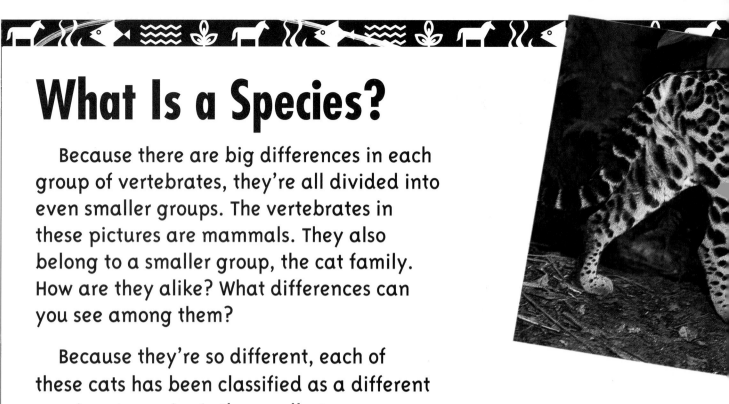

Because there are big differences in each group of vertebrates, they're all divided into even smaller groups. The vertebrates in these pictures are mammals. They also belong to a smaller group, the cat family. How are they alike? What differences can you see among them?

Because they're so different, each of these cats has been classified as a different species. A species is the smallest classification group, and its members can mate and produce young.

Scientific name:
Felis concolor
Common names:
cougar
puma
mountain lion
panther
catamount

Scientific name:
  Felis pardalis
Common name:
  ocelot

Every species that has ever been classified has its very own scientific name in Latin, an ancient language. The first part of the name is often shared with other species that are very similar. The last part of the name is the name of the species. No matter what language a scientist speaks, the scientist uses the scientific Latin name.

Each species also has a common name. In fact, many species have more than one common name. How could that be a problem?

Scientific name:
  Felis rufus
Common names:
  bobcat
  bay lynx

THINK!
How is it helpful for scientists all over the world to use the same scientific name for each organism?

How Do Members of the Same Species Vary?

All African elephants belong to the same species, *Loxodonta africana.* They have bigger bodies and bigger ears than Asian elephants, *Elephas maximus.* But do all African elephants look alike? What differences can you see between members of this herd?

Even if members of the same species look alike, each member is really different from all others. For people, one thing that's different is their fingerprints.

You need:
White paper
Pencil
Clear tape
Hand lens

Take a thumbprint test.

1 On paper, draw a dark black spot about the size of a quarter. Rub your thumb on the spot.

2 Stick a piece of clear tape on your thumb. Then stick the tape on a piece of white paper.

3 Examine your thumbprint. Compare it with one of the three main fingerprint patterns below.

4 Make a class table of thumbprints to see all the differences within each of the three types.

Fingerprints can be classified, just as organisms, groceries, and school supplies can. Did any two people have exactly the same thumbprints?

Arch

Loop

Whorl

THINK!
How do family members recognize each other in a big group?

How Would You Classify Living Things?

In almost any park, zoo, or aquarium you visit, there'll be some species from every kingdom. But you won't be able to see them all. Why not? How would you classify the living things in this picture?

Classify that organism.

❶ On the ThinkMat, give every organism a number or a letter.

❷ Divide the kingdoms into smaller and smaller groups. Keep going until you get to the species. Draw a table to show how your classification system works. Make up names for all the groups.

❸ Share your system with your classmates. How many different groups did people make for each kingdom?

You need:
ThinkMat 17
Paper
Markers
Trading cards

Grasslands, forests, deserts, and the ocean have species from every kingdom. Scientists classify members of the plant and fungi kingdoms into smaller groups the same way they do animals. How are all the species in each kingdom related to one another?

If you found a new organism someplace, how would you begin to figure out what it's related to?

Arthropod
Arthropods are invertebrates with exoskeletons and three or more pairs of jointed legs. About three-fourths of all animals are arthropods.

Characteristic
Characteristics are the ways by which you describe and classify things. You might describe something by color or shape, by the way it moves, or by what it's used for.

Cold-blooded
Cold-blooded means having a body temperature that changes with the temperatures of surrounding air or water. Most animals are cold-blooded.

Exoskeleton
An exoskeleton is the hard outside covering of an animal that has no skeleton inside its body.

Fungi kingdom
The fungi are a kingdom of simple organisms that absorb food from the material they live on. Yeasts, molds, and mushrooms are fungi.

Insect
Insects are arthropods with three main body parts—at least one pair of wings, a pair of antennae, and three pairs of legs.

Invertebrate
An invertebrate is an animal without a backbone or an internal skeleton. More than nine-tenths of all animals are invertebrates.